Horse Lovers Scroll Saw Projects

by
John A. Nelson

Fox Chapel Publishing Co., Inc.
1970 Broad Street
East Petersburg, PA 17520

John Nelson and other scrollers throughout the country have teamed up with Fox Chapel Publishing Company, Inc., to create a series of wonderful scroll saw books. This set of books is reasonably priced in order that scrollers can compile a great collection of scroll saw patterns and projects at a minimum cost. (In most cases less than twenty five cents per pattern.)

If you purchase—and like—any one book in this set of books, you should look at other books in the series, as we think you will want the other books as well.

The following people have my gratitude for helping with this book. Without them all this book could never have been published. First of all, to my wife Joyce, who interpreted my horrible writing and poor spelling. She turned my "hen scratching" into an actual manuscript for this book. To Hilary, my ten-year-old granddaughter, for helping Joyce paint many projects. Also, to Bill Ray of Akron, Ohio, and Paul Revere of Florida for helping me make many of the projects. Alan Giagnocavo and staff at Fox Chapel Publishing Company, Inc., without their help this book could not have been published.

I would like to acknowledge and thank those of you who have purchased my book. I sincerely hope you will enjoy our efforts.

John A. Nelson
PO Box 422
Dublin, NH 03444–0422

Publisher: Alan Giagnocavo
Project Editor: Ayleen Stellhorn

ISBN 1–56523–109–0

To order your copy of this book,
please send check or money order
for $9.95 plus $2.50 shipping to:
Fox Chapel Book Orders
1970 Broad Street
East Petersburg, PA 17520

Try your favorite book supplier first!

Table of Contents

Basic Instructions

In choosing the wood, be sure to choose an interesting piece of wood, a piece of wood with character and a nice grain pattern to it. (Remember, the _wood_ is the _least_ expensive part of your project --- it is your _time_ cutting and finishing the project that is the actual "cost".)

After carefully choosing wood for your project, cut the wood to overall size.

Sand the top and bottom surfaces with medium sandpaper. Finish up with fine sandpaper.

Make a copy of the pattern at a local copy center. Enlarge or reduce as noted on the drawing.

Because of size limitations, some of the larger patterns had to be cut in half. Simply make copies full-size or enlarged as noted, and line up the two halves and glue them back together. Take care to line up all matching lines. _Note_: Glue matching letters together, i.e., "X" to "X" and "Y" to "Y", etc.

Attach the pattern to the wood by spraying the pattern with a spray adhesive. Spray the back of the paper _not_ the wood. Let the adhesive set for a minute or two then attach pattern to the wood.

If there are interior cuts, carefully drill small starter holes for the blade to fit through, in each of the interior open areas. Carefully, make all interior cuts. (A #2 or #5 skip-tooth blade is recommended.) Be sure to keep a good sharp corners as you cut. Carefully, make the final outside cut.

Finishing

Sand all over with medium than fine sandpaper. Remove all dust from your project.

If you have to stain your project, try dipping it into a large, flat pan filled with the stain. Remove project and wipe down any excessive stain. (Pour the remaining stain back into the can for later use.) After stain dries, spray with satin or gloss varnish or lacquer, as noted above.

A few projects call for a plastic mirror as a background, simply cut the plastic as you do the wood. Glue in place.

After I have finished a project, I always put a coat of paste wax on the project. This gives your project a nice finish and "feel" to it.

Note: The projects in this book illustrates only one use of each project. Do not limit yourself only to what is suggested, try enlarging or reducing each project, change or modify the designs to create your very own project. You are limited only by your own imagination, experiment - have fun with these patterns.

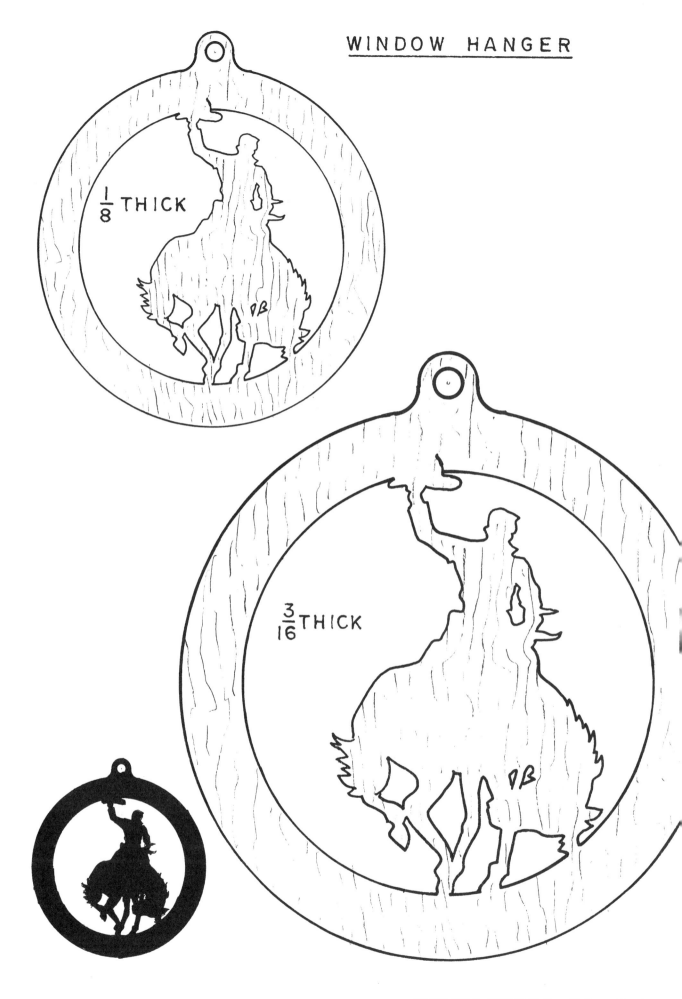

$\frac{1}{8}$ THICK

$\frac{3}{16}$ THICK

WINDOW HANGER

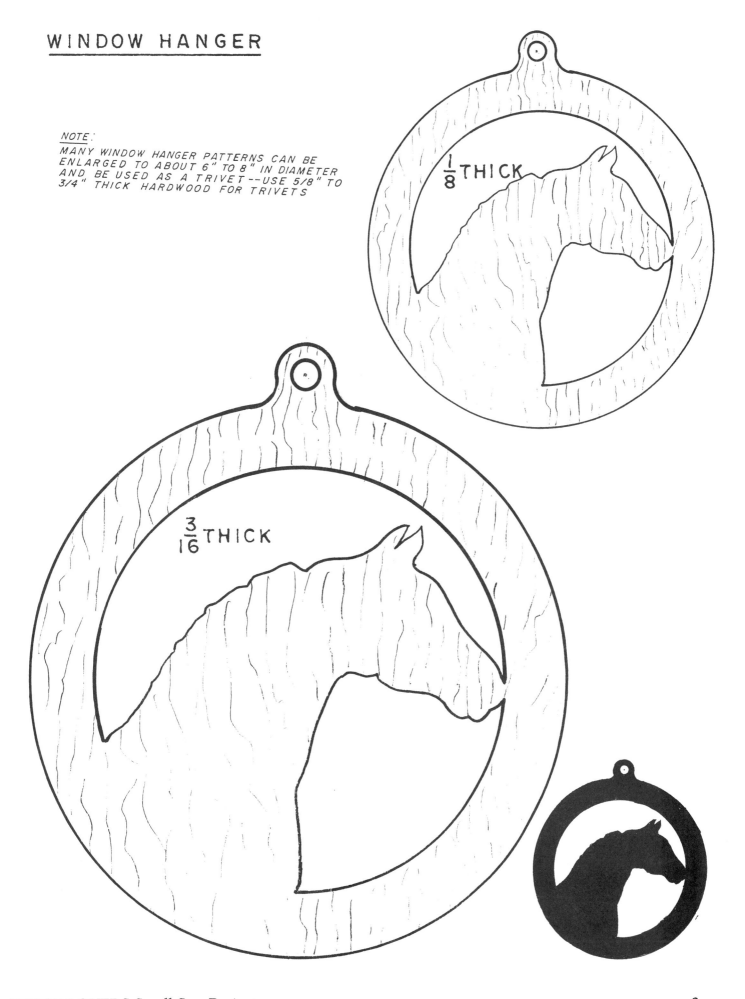

NOTE:
MANY WINDOW HANGER PATTERNS CAN BE
ENLARGED TO ABOUT 6" TO 8" IN DIAMETER
AND BE USED AS A TRIVET--USE 5/8" TO
3/4" THICK HARDWOOD FOR TRIVETS

$\frac{1}{8}$ THICK

$\frac{3}{16}$ THICK

WINDOW HANGER

NOTE:
MANY WINDOW HANGER PATTERNS CAN BE
ENLARGED TO ABOUT 6" TO 8" IN DIAMETER
AND BE USED AS A TRIVET--USE 5/8" TO
3/4" THICK HARDWOOD FOR TRIVETS

$\frac{1}{8}$ THICK

$\frac{3}{16}$ THICK

HORSE LOVERS Scroll Saw Projects

WINDOW HANGER

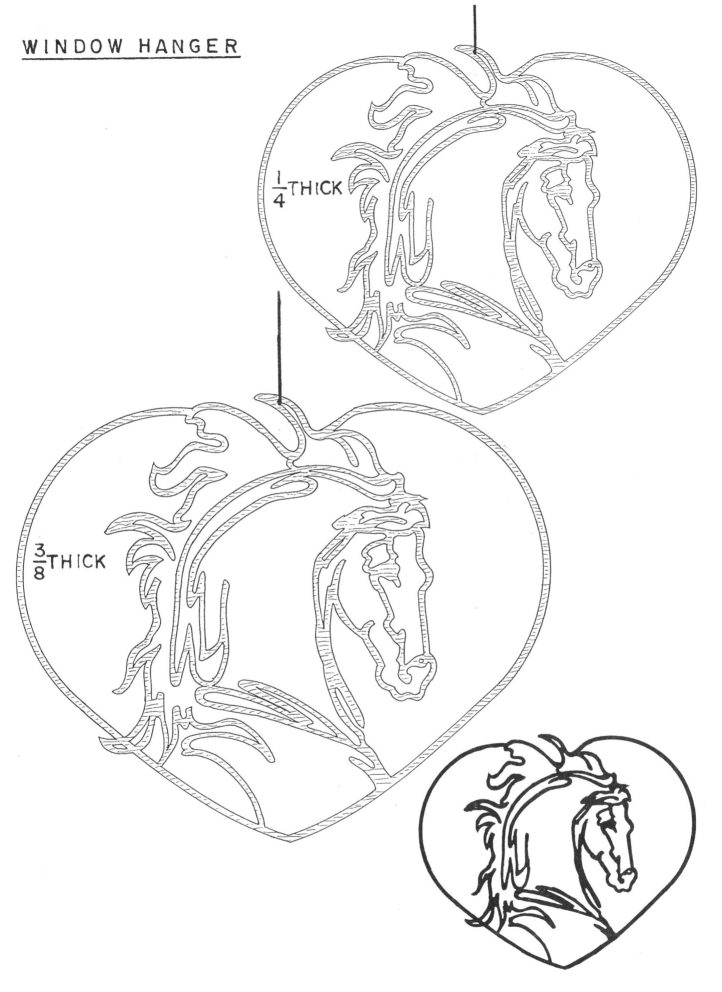

$\frac{1}{4}$ THICK

$\frac{3}{8}$ THICK

WALL CLOCK

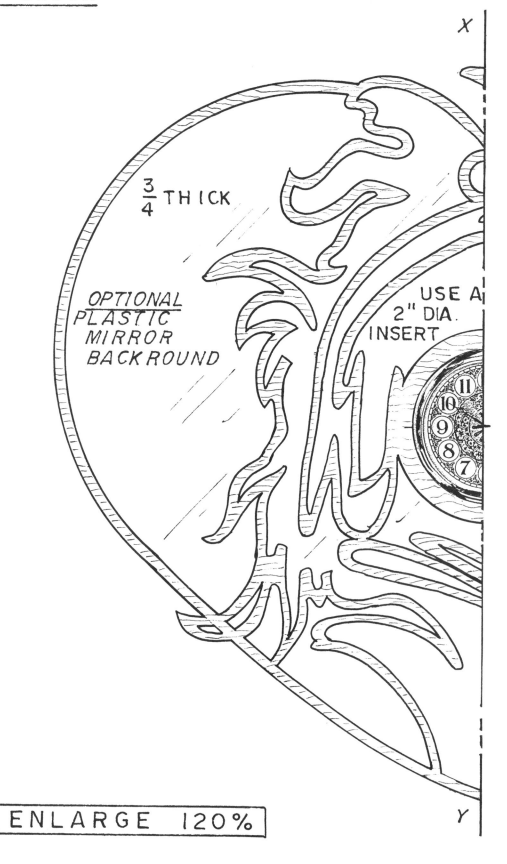

3/4 THICK

OPTIONAL
PLASTIC
MIRROR
BACKROUND

USE A
2" DIA.
INSERT

ENLARGE 120%

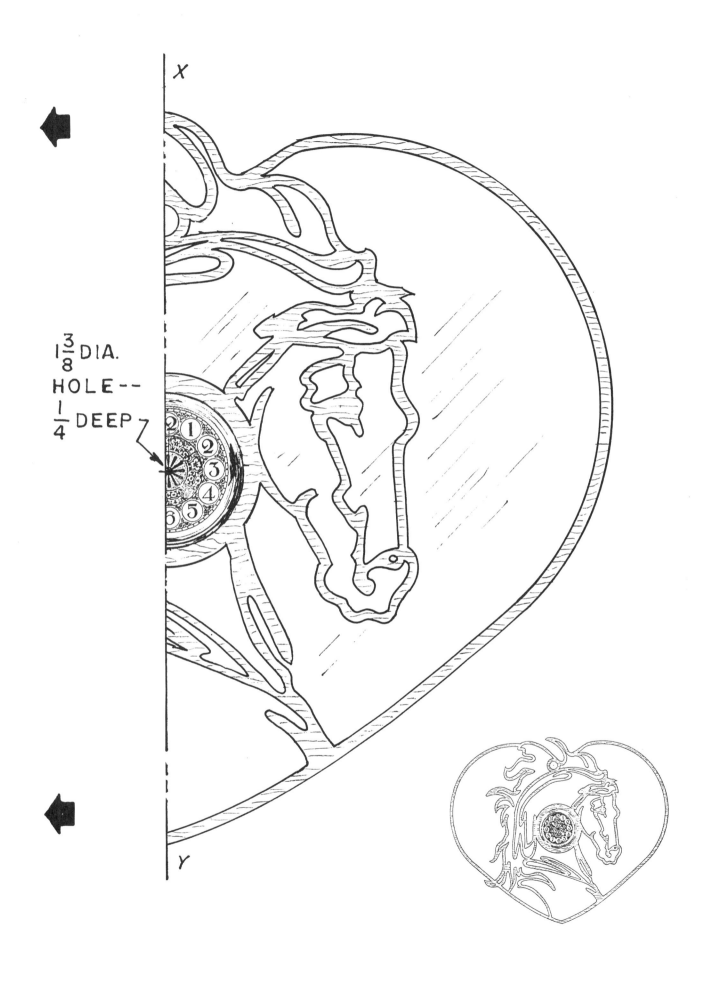

X

$1\frac{3}{8}$ DIA.
HOLE --
$\frac{1}{4}$ DEEP

Y

WALL CLOCK AND THEROMETER

SEE PAGE 11

SEE PAGE 12

SEE PAGE 13

SEE PAGE 14

WALL CLOCK AND THEROMETER

SEE PAGE 15

SEE PAGE 16

SEE PAGE 17

SEE PAGE 18

SEE PAGE 19

SEE PAGE 20

SEE PAGE 21

SEE PAGE 22

WALL CLOCK AND THERMOMETER

ENLARGE 130 %

MAT'L: 1/2 X 8 - 9 1/4

BRASS HANGER

1 7/16 DIA. HOLE - 5/16 DP.

THERMOMETER 1 7/16 DIA.

FIT-UP CLOCK 1 7/16 DIA.

WALL CLOCK AND THERMOMETER

ENLARGE 130%

MAT'L: 1/2 X 8 - 9 1/4

BRASS HANGER

1 7/16 DIA. HOLE - 5/16 DP.

THERMOMETER 1 7/16 DIA.

FIT-UP CLOCK 1 7/16 DIA.

WALL CLOCK AND THERMOMETER

ENLARGE 130%

MAT'L : 1/2 X 8 - 9 1/4

BRASS HANGER

1 7/16 DIA. HOLE - 5/16 DP.

THERMOMETER 1 7/16 DIA.

FIT-UP CLOCK 1 7/16 DIA.

WALL CLOCK AND THERMOMETER

ENLARGE 130%

MAT'L : 1/2 X 8 – 9 1/4

BRASS HANGER

1 7/16 DIA. HOLE – 5/16 DP.

THERMOMETER 1 7/16 DIA.
FIT-UP CLOCK 1 7/16 DIA.

WALL CLOCK AND THERMOMETER

ENLARGE 130%

MAT'L: 1/2 X 8 - 9 1/4

BRASS HANGER

1 7/16 DIA. HOLE - 5/16 DP.

THERMOMETER 1 7/16 DIA.
FIT-UP CLOCK 1 7/16 DIA.

WALL CLOCK AND THERMOMETER

ENLARGE 130%

MAT'L : 1/2 X 8 - 9 1/4

BRASS HANGER

1 7/16 DIA. HOLE - 5/16 DP.

THERMOMETER 1 7/16 DIA.

FIT-UP CLOCK 1 7/16 DIA.

WALL CLOCK AND THERMOMETER

ENLARGE 130%

MAT'L: 1/2 X 8 - 9 1/4

BRASS HANGER

1 7/16 DIA. HOLE - 5/16 DP.

THERMOMETER 1 7/16 DIA.

FIT-UP CLOCK 1 7/16 DIA.

WALL CLOCK AND THERMOMETER

ENLARGE 130%

MAT'L: 1/2 X 8 - 9 1/4

BRASS HANGER

1 7/16 DIA. HOLE - 5/16 DP.

THERMOMETER 1 7/16 DIA.

FIT-UP CLOCK 1 7/16 DIA.

WALL CLOCK AND THERMOMETER

ENLARGE 130%

MAT'L: 1/2 X 8 - 9 1/4

BRASS HANGER

1 7/16 DIA. HOLE - 5/16 DP.

THERMOMETER 1 7/16 DIA.

FIT-UP CLOCK 1 7/16 DIA.

WALL CLOCK AND THERMOMETER

ENLARGE 130%

MAT'L: 1/2 X 8 - 9 1/4

BRASS HANGER

I 7/16 DIA. HOLE -5/16 DP.

THERMOMETER I 7/16 DIA.

FIT-UP CLOCK I 7/16 DIA.

HORSE LOVERS Scroll Saw Projects

WALL CLOCK AND THERMOMETER

ENLARGE 130 %

MAT'L : 1/2 X 8 - 9 1/4

BRASS HANGER

1 7/16 DIA. HOLE - 5/16 DP.

THERMOMETER 1 7/16 DIA.

FIT-UP CLOCK 1 7/16 DIA.

WALL CLOCK AND THERMOMETER

ENLARGE 130 %

MAT'L : 1/2 X 8 - 9 1/4

BRASS HANGER

1 7/16 DIA. HOLE - 5/16 DP.

THERMOMETER 1 7/16 DIA.
FIT-UP CLOCK 1 7/16 DIA.

PLANT-MATE CLOCK

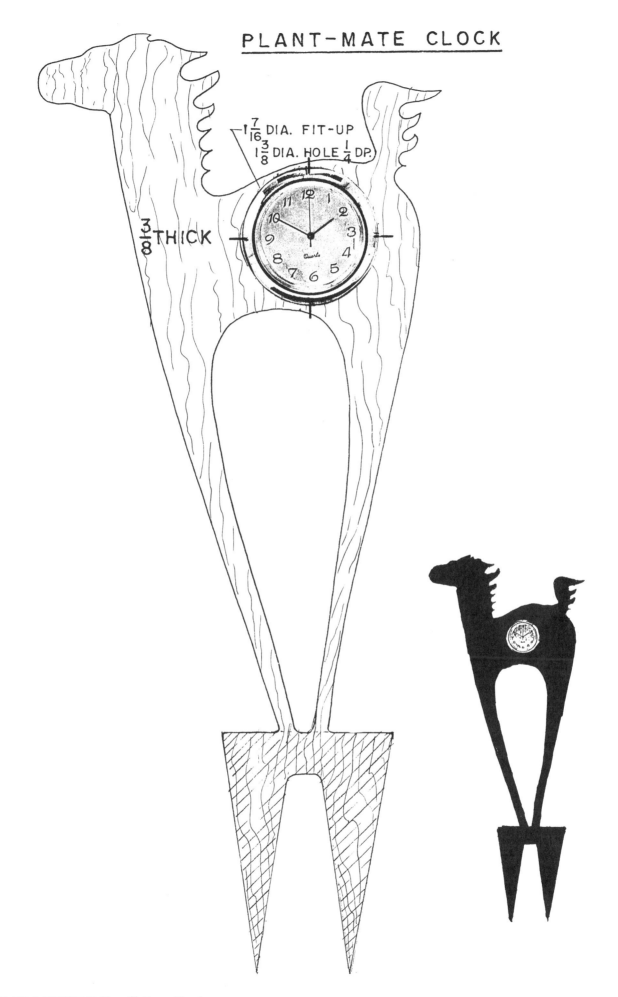

$1\frac{7}{16}$ DIA. FIT-UP

$1\frac{3}{8}$ DIA. HOLE $\frac{1}{4}$ DP.

$\frac{3}{8}$ THICK

WALL SHELF

1/4 DIA. HOLE
3 PLACES

BRACE

MAT'L.
1/4 X 8 1/4 - 12 1/4

FRONT VIEW

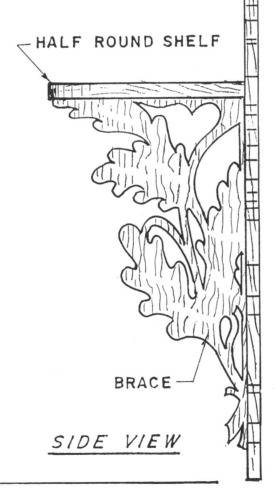

ENLARGE 125%

HALF ROUND SHELF

BRACE

SIDE VIEW

WALL SHELF

1/4 DIA. HOLE
3 PLACES

BRACE

MAT'L.
1/4 X 8 1/4 - 12 1/4

FRONT VIEW

HORSE LOVERS Scroll Saw Projects

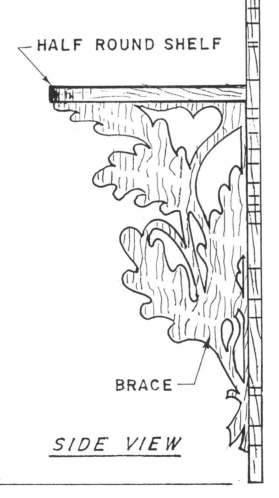

ENLARGE 125%

HALF ROUND SHELF

BRACE

SIDE VIEW

WALL SHELF

1/4 DIA. HOLE
- 3 PLACES

BRACE

MAT'L.
1/4 X 8 1/4 - 12 1/4

FRONT VIEW

ENLARGE 125%

— HALF ROUND SHELF

BRACE

SIDE VIEW

HORSE LOVERS Scroll Saw Projects

29

WALL SHELF

1/4 DIA. HOLE
3 PLACES

BRACE

MAT'L.
1/4 X 8 1/4 — 12 1/4

FRONT VIEW

ENLARGE 125%

HALF ROUND SHELF

BRACE

SIDE VIEW

WALL SHELF

1/4 DIA. HOLE

HALF ROUND SHELF

SHAPE OF BRACE

BRACE

1/64 DIA. HOLE 6 PLACES

ENLARGE 130 %

32

HORSE LOVERS Scroll Saw Projects

WALL SHELF

1/4 DIA. HOLE

HALF ROUND SHELF

1/64 DIA. HOLE
6 PLACES

BRACE

SHAPE OF BRACE

ENLARGE 130%

HORSE LOVERS Scroll Saw Projects

WALL SHELF

1/4 DIA. HOLE

HALF ROUND SHELF

SHAPE OF BRACE

BRACE

1/64 DIA. HOLE
6 PLACES

ENLARGE 130%

HORSE LOVERS Scroll Saw Projects

WALL CLOCK

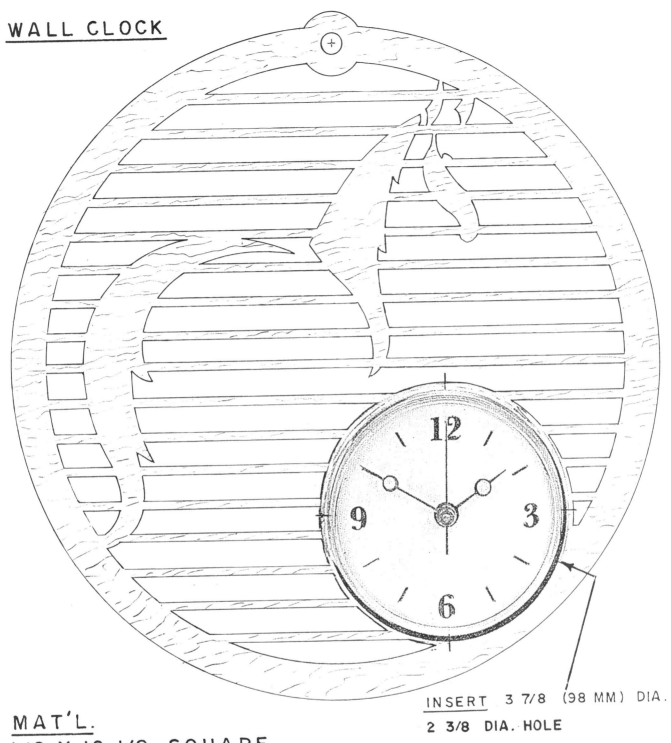

INSERT 3 7/8 (98 MM) DIA.

2 3/8 DIA. HOLE

MAT'L.
1/2 X 10 1/2 SQUARE

ENLARGE 150%

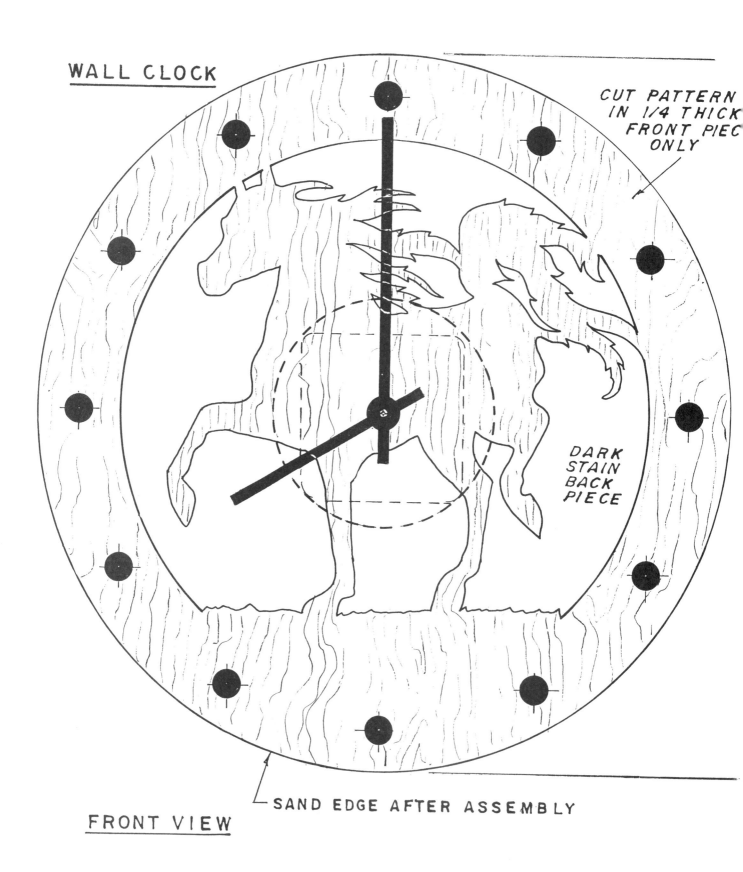

CUT PATTERN
IN 1/4 THICK
FRONT PIEC
ONLY

DARK
STAIN
BACK
PIECE

SAND EDGE AFTER ASSEMBLY

FRONT VIEW

HORSE LOVERS Scroll Saw Projects

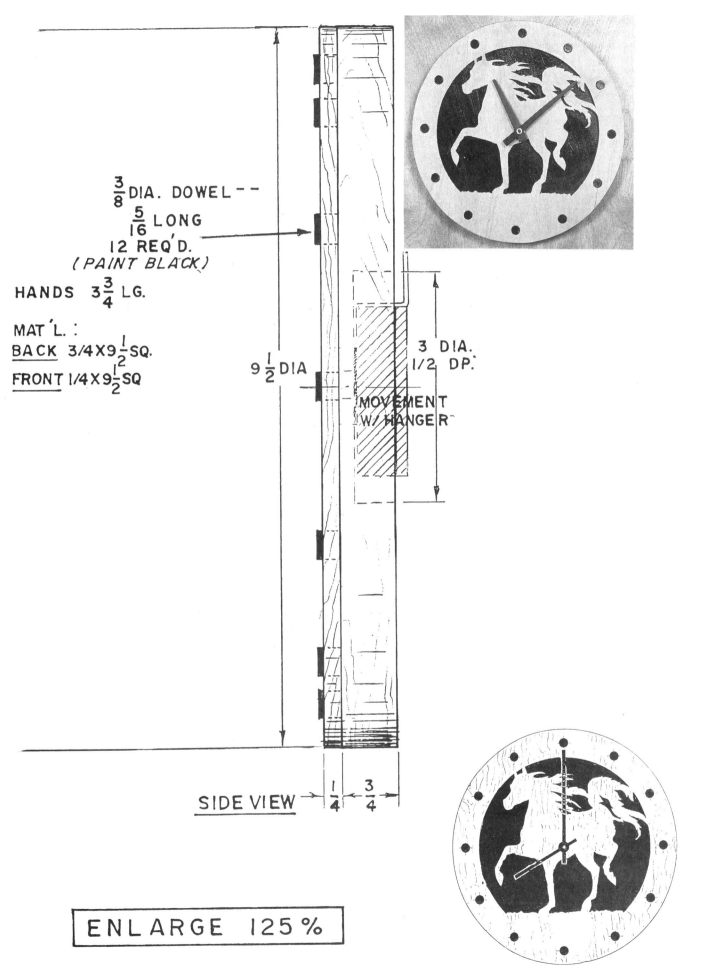

$\frac{3}{8}$ DIA. DOWEL --
$\frac{5}{16}$ LONG
12 REQ'D.
(PAINT BLACK)

HANDS $3\frac{3}{4}$ LG.

MAT'L. :
BACK 3/4 X 9$\frac{1}{2}$ SQ.
FRONT 1/4 X 9$\frac{1}{2}$ SQ

9$\frac{1}{2}$ DIA

3 DIA.
1/2 DP.

MOVEMENT
W/ HANGER

SIDE VIEW

$\frac{1}{4}$ $\frac{3}{4}$

ENLARGE 125%

HORSE LOVERS Scroll Saw Projects

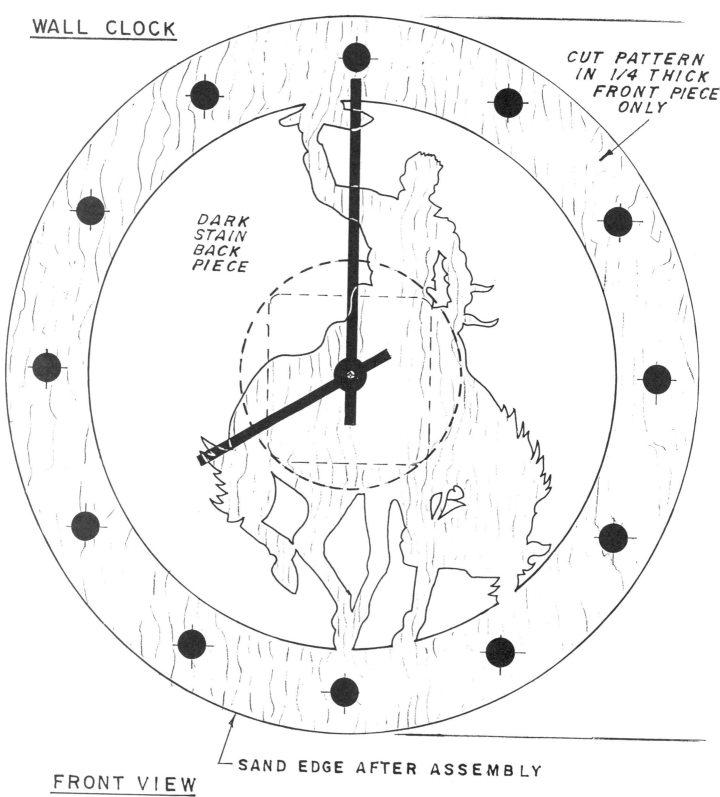

CUT PATTERN
IN 1/4 THICK
FRONT PIECE
ONLY

DARK
STAIN
BACK
PIECE

SAND EDGE AFTER ASSEMBLY

FRONT VIEW

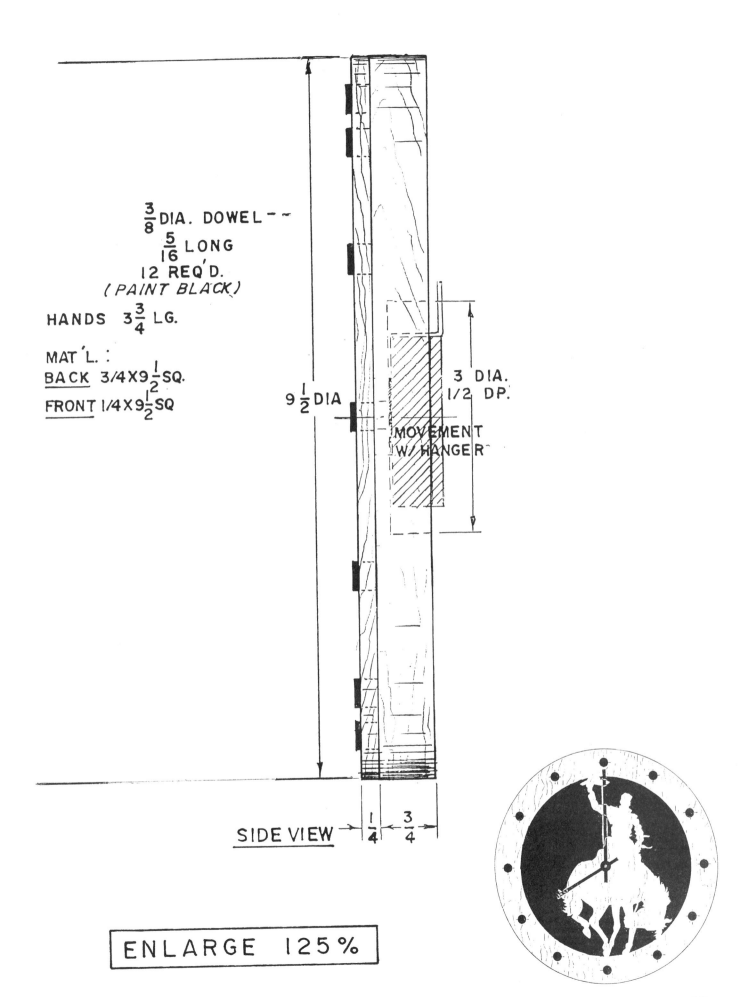

$\frac{3}{8}$ DIA. DOWEL -- ~

$\frac{5}{16}$ LONG

12 REQ'D.

(PAINT BLACK)

HANDS $3\frac{3}{4}$ LG.

MAT'L.:

BACK 3/4X9$\frac{1}{2}$SQ.

FRONT 1/4X9$\frac{1}{2}$SQ

$9\frac{1}{2}$ DIA

3 DIA.

1/2 DP.

MOVEMENT

W/ HANGER

SIDE VIEW

$\frac{1}{4}$ $\frac{3}{4}$

ENLARGE 125%

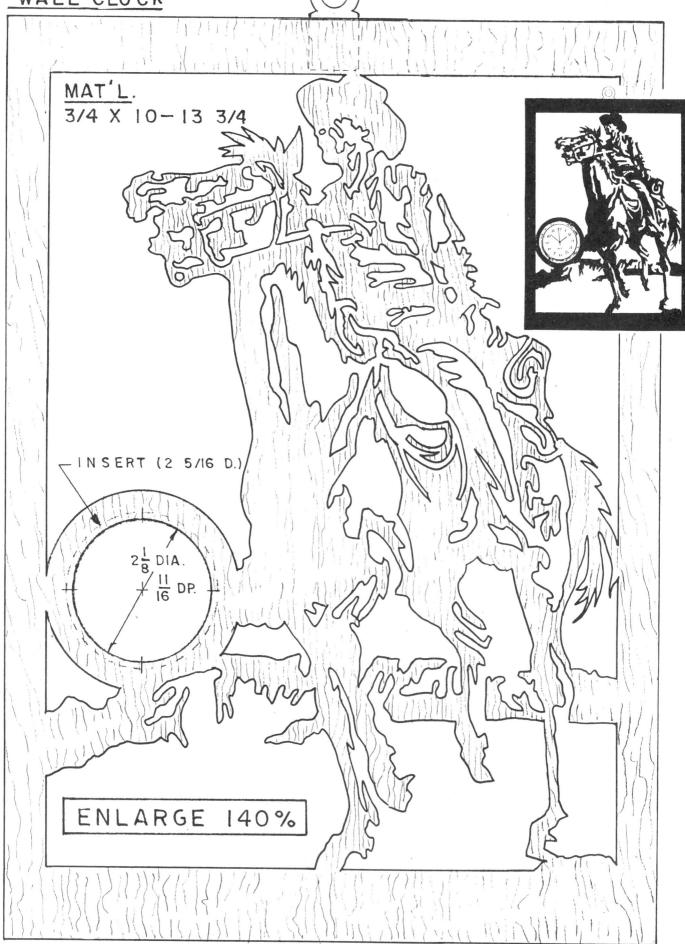

MAT'L.
3/4 X 10 — 13 3/4

INSERT (2 5/16 D.)

$2\frac{1}{8}$ DIA.
$\frac{11}{16}$ DP.

ENLARGE 140%

MIRROR WALL PLAQUE

(PLACE MIRROR BEHIND WOOD)

ENLARGE 160%

MATL. 5/8 X 9 1/4 – 14 1/4

WALL CLOCK

$2\frac{3}{8}$ DIA.
HOLE --
$\frac{11}{16}$ DEEP →

INSERT 4 DIA.

MAT'L.
3/4 X 8 1/4 — 15
OPTIONAL
MIRROR BACKING

ENLARGE
165 %

HORSE LOVERS Scroll Saw Projects

WALL CLOCK
& BAROMETER

MAT'L.
3/4 X 8 1/2 –
15 3/4
*OPTIONAL
CLOTH BACKING*

ENLARGE
170 %

$2\frac{3}{8}$ DIA. HOLE
2 PLACES

$2\frac{3}{4}$ DIA.

ROUND WALL CLOCK

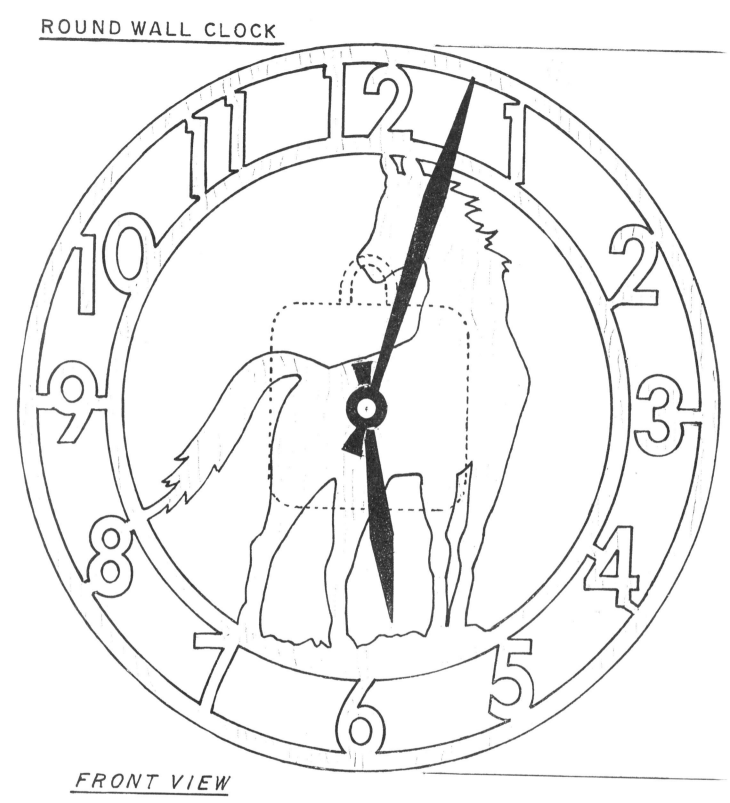

FRONT VIEW

SUGGESTION:
TRY ADDING MIRRORED PLEXIGLAS TO THE
BACK OF THIS PROJECT — COLOR TO SUIT.

HORSE LOVERS Scroll Saw Projects

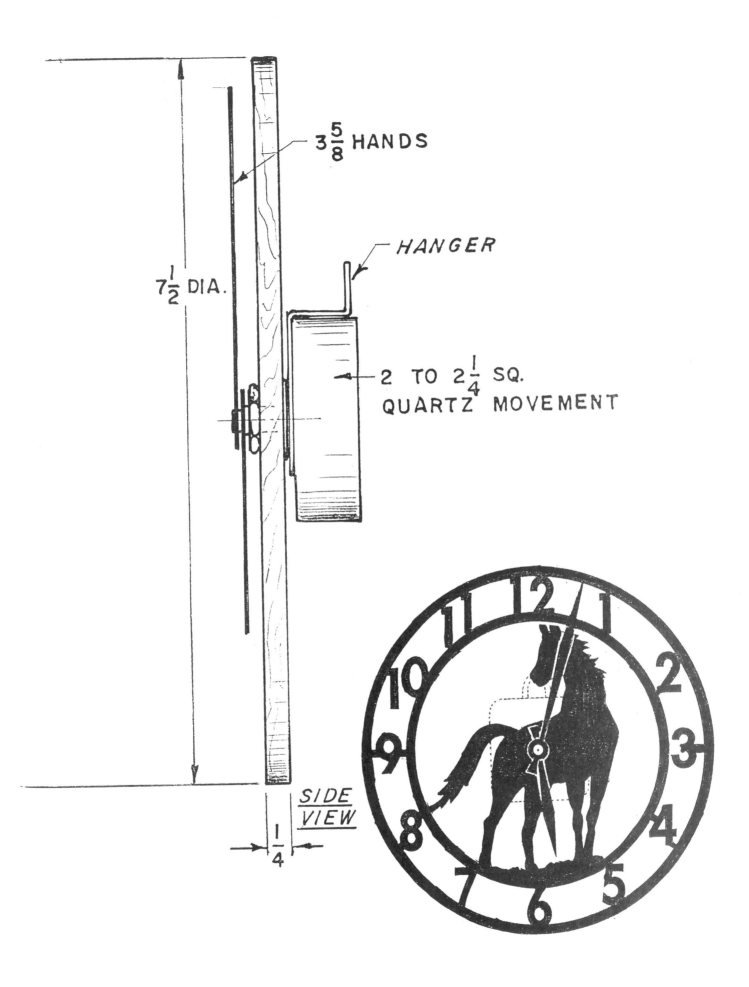

$3\frac{5}{8}$ HANDS

HANGER

$7\frac{1}{2}$ DIA.

2 TO $2\frac{1}{4}$ SQ.
QUARTZ MOVEMENT

SIDE
VIEW

$\frac{1}{4}$

ROUND WALL CLOCK

FRONT VIEW

HORSE LOVERS Scroll Saw Projects

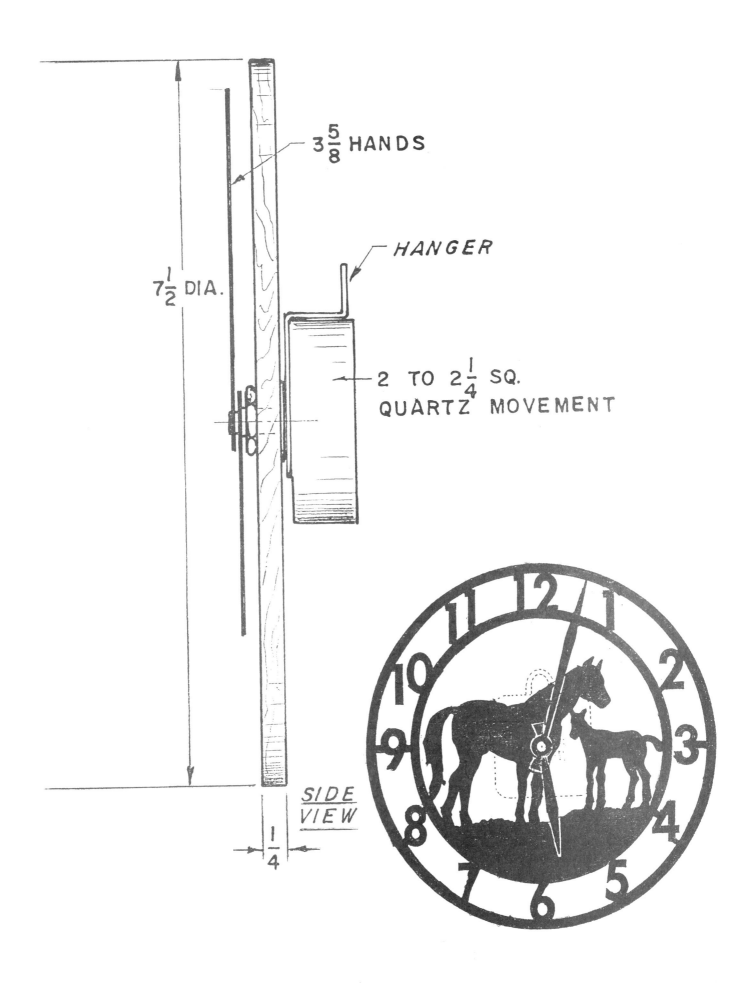

$3\frac{5}{8}$ HANDS

HANGER

$7\frac{1}{2}$ DIA.

2 TO $2\frac{1}{4}$ SQ.
QUARTZ MOVEMENT

SIDE
VIEW

$\frac{1}{4}$

WALL PLAQUE

X

Y

MAT'L.
1/2 X 9 3/4 – 14 3/4
PLASTIC MIRROR BACKING

WALL SHELF
W/DRAWER
C. 1890

FRONT VIEW

SIDE VIEW

1/3 LIP
TOP EDGE

FLUSH AT BOTTOM

ASSEMBLY VIEW

SEE PAGE 52

C   D

HORSE LOVERS Scroll Saw Projects

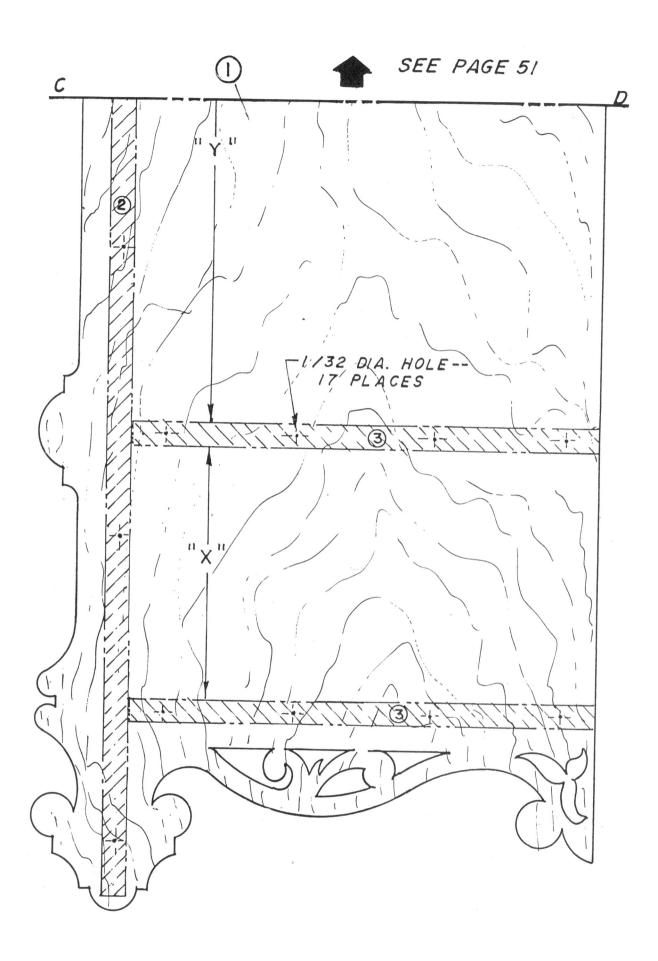

SEE PAGE 51

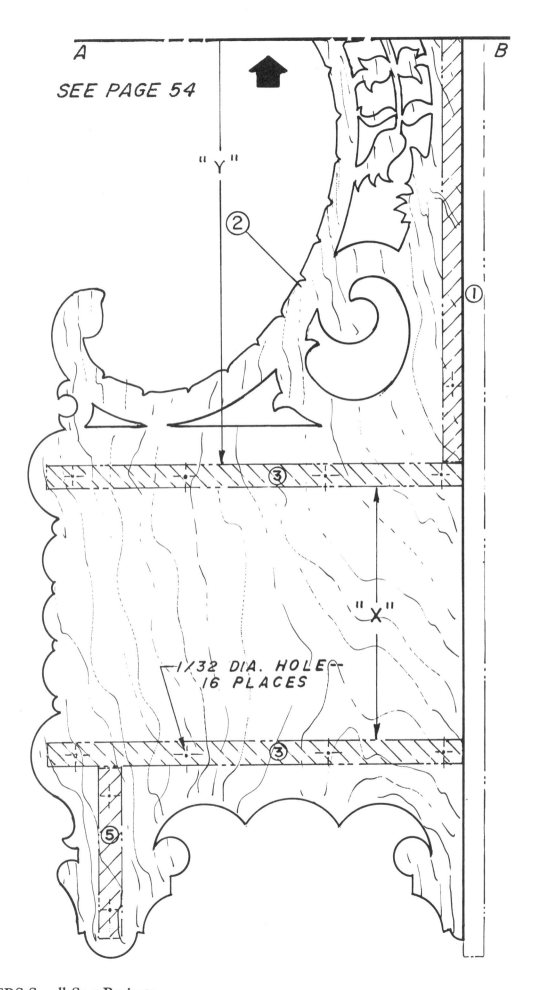

A   B

SEE PAGE 54

"Y"

②

①

③

"X"

1/32 DIA. HOLE
16 PLACES

③

⑤

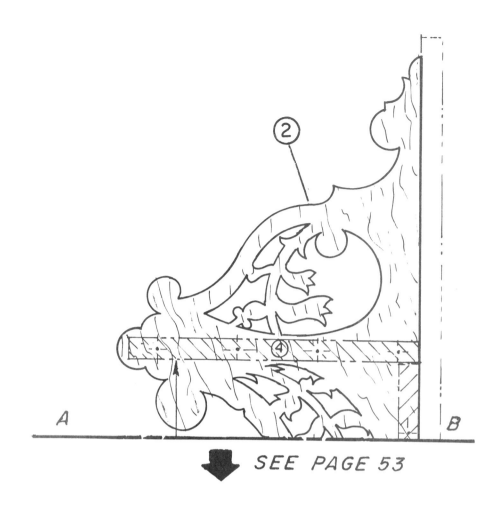

SEE PAGE 53

NO.	NAME	SIZE	REQ'D.
1	BACK BOARD ✱	1/4 X 6 1/8 – 16 1/4	2
2	SIDE	1/4 X 4 3/4 – 14 1/2	2
3	SHELF	1/4 X 4 5/8 – 10	2
4	SHELF-TOP	1/4 X 3 1/4 –10	1
5	TRIM-BOTTOM	1/4 X 1 3/4 –10	1
6	BACK PICTURE	1/4 X 5 1/4 –10	1
7	DRAWER-FACE	1/4 X 2 5/8 – 10	1
8	DRAWER-FRONT/BACK	1/4 X 2 1/4 – 9 1/2	2
9	DRAWER-END	1/4 X 2 1/2 – 4	2
10	DRAWER-BOTTOM	1/4 X 4 – 9 1/2	1
11	DRAWER PULL	1/2 DIA.	1
12	BRAD	5/8 LONG	AS REQ'D
✱	NOTE: THE ORIGIONAL WAS MADE IN TWO		
	PIECES AND NOT GLUED TOGETHER		

1/32 DIA. HOLE

HORSE LOVERS Scroll Saw Projects

USE A LIGHTER
OR
DARKER STAIN
(OPTIONAL)

⑥

Appendix 'A'

Where To Get Clock Parts and Hardware

(These are the names/addresses we know of at this time any omissions
are only because we do not know of them or simply we "goofed".) Write
them for their catalog - tell them the NELSON'S of "NELSON DESIGNS"
told you to write them.

In Alphabet Order:

Amor Crafts
PO Box 445
East Northport, NY 11731

Cherry Tree
PO Box 369
Belmont, OH 43718

Constantine
2050 Eastchester Road
Bronx, NY 10461

Don Jer Products (Suede-Tex-only)
8 Ilene Court
Belle Mead, NJ 08502

Innovation Specialties
11869 Teale Street
Culver City, CA 90230

Klockit
PO Box 636
Lake Geneva, WI 53145

Leichtung Workshops
1 Woodworkers Way
Seabrook, NH 03874

Meisel Hardware Specialties
PO Box 70
Mound, MN 55364-0070

Merritt Antiques, Inc.
RD 2
Douglasville, PA 19518

Precision Movements
4251 Chestnut Street PO Box 689
Emmaus, PA 18049-0689

P.S. Wood
10 Dowing Street Suite #3
Library, PA 15129

S. LaRose, Inc.
234 Commerce Place
Greensborough, NC 27420

Shipley Co.
2075 S. University Blvd. Suite 119
Denver, CO 80210

Sloan's Woodshop
3453 Callis Road
Lebanon, TN 37090

Steebar Corp.
PO Box 980
Andover, NJ 07821-0980

Turncraft
PO Box 70
Mound, TN 55364-0070

Woodcraft
PO Box 4000 41 Atlantic Ave.
Woburn, MA 01888

Woodworkers Supply of New Mexico
5604 Alameda NE
Albuquerque, NM 87113